HOW CAN I PRACTICE
CHRISTIAN MEDITATION?

✕ CULTIVATING BIBLICAL GODLINESS

Series Editors

Joel R. Beeke and Ryan M. McGraw

Dr. D. Martyn Lloyd-Jones once said that what the church needs to do most of all is "to begin herself to live the Christian life. If she did that, men and women would be crowding into our buildings. They would say, 'What is the secret of this?'" As Christians, one of our greatest needs is for the Spirit of God to cultivate biblical godliness in us in order to put the beauty of Christ on display through us, all to the glory of the triune God. With this goal in mind, this series of booklets treats matters vital to Christian experience at a basic level. Each booklet addresses a specific question in order to inform the mind, warm the affections, and transform the whole person by the Spirit's grace, so that the church may adorn the doctrine of God our Savior in all things.

HOW CAN I PRACTICE
CHRISTIAN MEDITATION?

JOEL R. BEEKE

REFORMATION HERITAGE BOOKS
GRAND RAPIDS, MICHIGAN

How Can I Practice Christian Meditation?
© 2016 by Joel R. Beeke

Reformation Heritage Books
2965 Leonard St. NE
Grand Rapids, MI 49525
616-977-0889 / Fax 616-285-3246
orders@heritagebooks.org
www.heritagebooks.org

Printed in the United States of America
16 17 18 19 20 21/10 9 8 7 6 5 4 3 2 1

ISBN 978-1-60178-491-9

For additional Reformed literature, request a free book list from Reformation Heritage Books at the above regular or e-mail address.

HOW CAN I PRACTICE
CHRISTIAN MEDITATION?

———✖———

Spiritual growth is intended to be part of the Christian life of believers.[1] Peter exhorts believers to "grow in grace, and in the knowledge of our Lord and Saviour Jesus Christ" (2 Peter 3:18). True Christians are members of Christ by faith and partake in His anointing. By Christ's power they are raised up to a new life and have the Holy Spirit given to them as an earnest, by whose power they "seek those things which are above" (Col. 3:1). Spiritual growth is only to be expected since "it is impossible that those, who are implanted into Christ by a true faith, should not bring forth fruits of thankfulness" (Heidelberg Catechism, Q. 32, 45, 49, 64).

One hindrance to growth among Christians today is their failure to cultivate spiritual knowledge

---

1. This booklet is adapted from Joel R. Beeke, "The Puritan Practice of Meditation," in Joel R. Beeke and Mark Jones, *A Puritan Theology: Doctrine for Life* (Grand Rapids: Reformation Heritage Books, 2012), 889–907.

by meditation. We are conscious that we often fail to give enough time to Bible reading and prayer, but too often we fail to realize that, for the most part, we have abandoned altogether the practice of meditation. How tragic that the very word *meditation*, once regarded as a core discipline of Christianity and, according to Richard J. Foster, a "crucial preparation for and adjunct to the work of prayer" is now associated with unbiblical "New Age" spirituality. We rightly criticize those who engage in transcendental meditation and other mind-relaxing exercises because these practices are connected with false religions, such as Buddhism and Hinduism, and have nothing to do with Scripture. Such forms of meditation focus on emptying the mind to become detached from the world and to merge with the so-called Cosmic Mind. There is no living, personal God to attach to, to listen to, and to be active for. Yet, we can learn from such people the importance of quiet reflection and prolonged meditation.[2]

At one time, the Christian church was deeply engaged in biblical meditation, which involved detachment from sin and attachment to God and one's neighbor. In the Puritan age, numerous ministers preached and wrote on how to meditate. In this booklet, we will sit at the feet of the Puritans, considering what they taught about the nature,

---

2. Richard J. Foster, *Celebration of Discipline* (San Francisco: Harper & Row, 1978), 14–15.

duty, manner, subjects, benefits, obstacles, and self-examination of meditation.[3] By God's grace, with the Puritans as mentors, combined with holy resolve, perhaps we can recover the biblical practice of meditation for our time.

THE DEFINITION, NATURE, AND KINDS OF MEDITATION

"While I was musing the fire burned," David said (Ps. 39:3). The word *meditate* or *muse* means to "think on" or to "reflect." It also means "to murmur, to mutter, to make sound with the mouth.... It implies what we express by one talking to himself."[4] A person who practices this kind of meditation recites aloud a memorized passage of Scripture to himself in a low undertone.

The Bible often speaks of meditation. "Isaac went out to meditate in the field at the eventide," says Genesis 24:63. Even though the Lord gave Joshua the demanding task of supervising the conquest of Canaan, He commanded Joshua to meditate on the book of the law day and night so that he might do all that was written in it (Josh. 1:8). The term *meditation*,

---

3. For a recent study on the Puritan art of meditation, see David W. Saxton, *God's Battle Plan for the Mind: The Puritan Practice of Biblical Meditation* (Grand Rapids: Reformation Heritage Books, 2015). For a bibliography of other studies, see Beeke and Jones, *Puritan Theology*, 889–90n3.

4. William Wilson, *Old Testament Word Studies* (McLean, Va.: MacDonald Publishing, n.d.), 271.

however, occurs more often in the Psalms than in all other books of the Bible together. Psalm 1 calls that man blessed who delights in the law of the Lord and meditates on it day and night. In Psalm 63:6, David speaks of remembering the Lord on his bed and meditating on Him in the night watches. Psalm 119:148 says, "Mine eyes prevent the night watches, that I might meditate in thy word" (cf. Pss. 4:4; 77:10–12; 104:34; 119:15, 48, 59, 78, 97–99).

Thinking, reflecting, or musing presupposes something to meditate on. Formal meditation implies weighty subjects. For example, philosophers meditate on concepts such as matter and the universe, while theologians reflect on God, the eternal decrees, and the will of man.

The Puritans never tired of saying that biblical meditation involves thinking on the triune God and His Word. By anchoring meditation in the living Word, Jesus Christ, and God's written Word, the Bible, the Puritans distanced themselves from the kind of bogus spirituality or mysticism that stresses contemplation at the expense of action, and flights of the imagination at the expense of biblical content.

For the Puritans, meditation exercised both the mind and the heart; he who meditates approaches a subject with his intellect as well as his affections. Thomas Watson (c. 1620–1686) defined meditation as "a holy exercise of the mind whereby we bring the truths of God to remembrance, and do seriously ponder upon them and apply them to ourselves."[5]

Edmund Calamy (1600–1666) wrote, "A true meditation is when a man doth so meditate of Christ as to get his *heart* inflamed with the love of Christ; so meditate of the Truths of God, as to be transformed into them; and so meditate of sin as to get his heart to hate sin." Calamy went on to say that, to do good, meditation must enter three doors: the door of understanding, the door of the heart and affections, and the door of practical living. "Thou must so meditate of God as to walk as God walks; and so to meditate of Christ as to prize him, and live in obedience to him."[6]

For the Puritans, meditation was a daily duty that enhanced every other duty of the Christian life. As oil lubricates an engine, so meditation facilitates the diligent use of means of grace (reading of Scripture, hearing sermons, prayer, and all other ordinances of Christ; cf. Westminster Larger Catechism, Q. 154), deepens the marks of grace (repentance, faith,

---

5. Thomas Watson, *Heaven Taken by Storm* (Morgan, Pa.: Soli Deo Gloria, 2000), 23. For similar definitions by other Puritans, see Richard Greenham, "Grave Counsels and Godly Observations," in *The Works of the Reverend and Faithfull Servant of Jesus Christ M. Richard Greenham*, ed. H. H. (London: Felix Kingston for Robert Dexter, 1599), 37; Thomas Hooker, *The Application of Redemption … The Ninth and Tenth Books* (London: Peter Cole, 1657), 210; Thomas White, *A Method and Instructions for the Art of Divine Meditation with Instances of the Several Kindes of Solemn Meditation* (London: for Tho. Parkhurst, 1672), 13.

6. Edmund Calamy, *The Art of Divine Meditation* (London: for Tho. Parkhurst, 1634), 26–28.

humility), and strengthens one's relationships to others (love to God, to fellow Christians, to one's neighbors at large).

The Puritans wrote of two kinds of meditation: occasional and deliberate. "There is a *sudden, short, occasional meditation* of Heavenly things; and there is a *solemn, set, deliberate meditation*," Calamy wrote. Occasional meditation takes what one observes with the senses to "raise up his thoughts to Heavenly meditation." The believer makes use of what he sees with his eyes, or hears with his ears, "as a ladder to climb to Heaven." That's what David did with the moon and stars in Psalm 8, what Solomon did with the ants in Proverbs 6, and what Christ did with well water in John 4.[7] Thomas Manton (1620–1677) explained,

> God trained up the old church by types and ceremonies, that upon a common object they might ascend to spiritual thoughts; and our Lord in the new testament taught by parables and similitudes taken from ordinary functions and offices among men, that in every trade and calling we might be employed in our worldly business with an heavenly mind, that, whether in the shop, or at the loom, or in the field, we might still think of Christ and heaven.[8]

---

7. Calamy, *Art of Divine Meditation*, 6–10.

8. Thomas Manton, *The Works of Thomas Manton* (London: James Nisbet & Co., 1874), 17:267–68.

Nearly every Puritan book on meditation mentions occasional meditation. Some Puritans, such as William Spurstowe (c. 1605–1666) and Thomas Taylor (1576–1633), wrote entire books of occasional meditations.[9] Occasional meditation is relatively easy for a believer because it may be practiced at any time, any place, and among any people. A spiritually minded person can quickly learn how to spiritualize natural things, for his desires run counter to the worldly minded, who carnalize even spiritual things.[10] As Manton wrote, "A gracious heart is like an alembic [distillation apparatus], it can distil useful meditations out of all things it meeteth with. As it seeth all things in God, so it seeth God in all things."[11]

Occasional meditation had its dangers, however. Bishop Joseph Hall (1574–1656) warned that when left unbridled, such meditations could easily wander from the Word and become superstitious, as was the case in Roman Catholic spirituality.[12] One's imagination must be reined in by the Bible.

---

9. William Spurstowe, *The Spiritual Chymist: or, Six Decads Of Divine Meditations* (London: n.p., 1666); Thomas Taylor, *Meditations from the Creatures* (London: [H. Lownes] for I. Bartlet, 1629).

10. Calamy, *Art of Divine Meditation*, 14–15.

11. Manton, *Works*, 17:267. Cf. Thomas Watson: "A gracious heart, like fire, turns all objects into fuel for meditation," from *The Sermons of Thomas Watson* (Ligonier, Pa.: Soli Deo Gloria, 1990), 247.

12. Frank Livingstone Huntley, *Bishop Joseph Hall and Protestant Meditation in Seventeenth-Century England* (Binghamton, N.Y.: Center for Medieval & Early Renaissance Studies, 1981), 74.

The most important kind of meditation is daily, deliberate meditation, engaged in at set times. Calamy said deliberate meditation takes place "when a man *sets apart*...some time, and goes into a private Closet, or a private Walk, and there doth solemnly and *deliberately meditate of the things of Heaven*." Such deliberation dwells on God, Christ, and truth like "the Bee that dwells and abides upon the flower, to suck out all the sweetness." It is "a reflecting act of the soul, whereby the soul is carried back to itself, and considers all the things that it knows" about the subject, including its "causes, fruits, [and] properties."[13]

Thomas White (c. 1577–c. 1672) said deliberate meditation draws from four sources: Scripture, practical truths of Christianity, providential occasions (experiences), and sermons. Sermons in particular are fertile fields for meditation. As White wrote, "It is better to hear one Sermon only and meditate on that, than to hear two Sermons and meditate on neither."[14]

Some Puritans divided deliberate meditation into two parts: meditation that is direct and focuses on the meditated object and meditation that is reflective (or "reflexive") and focuses on the person who is meditating. Direct meditation is an act of the contemplative part of the understanding, whereas reflective meditation is an act of conscience. Direct meditation

---

13. Calamy, *Art of Divine Meditation*, 22–23; cf. Greenham, *Works*, 38.

14. White, *Method and Instructions for the Art of Divine Meditation*, 17–20.

enlightens the mind with knowledge, while reflective meditation fills the heart with goodness.

Deliberate meditation can be dogmatic, having the Word as its object, or practical, having our lives as its object.[15] Thomas Gouge (1605–1681) combined several aspects of deliberate meditation: "A set and deliberate Meditation, is a serious applying of the mind to some spiritual or heavenly subject, discoursing thereof with thy self, to the end thine heart may be warmed, thine affections quickened, and thy resolutions heightened to a greater love of God, hatred of sin, &c."[16]

Richard Baxter (1615–1691) said that "set and solemn" meditation differs from "occasional and cursory" meditation much as set times of prayer differ from spontaneous prayers uttered in the midst of daily business.[17] Both kinds of meditation are essential for godliness. They serve both the needs of the head and the heart.[18] Without heart application, meditation is no more than study. As Thomas Watson

---

15. Manton, *Works*, 17:268.

16. Thomas Gouge, *Christian Directions, Shewing How to Walk with God All the Day Long* (London: R. Ibbitson and M. Wright, 1661), 65.

17. Richard Baxter, *The Saints' Everlasting Rest* (repr., Fearn, Scotland: Christian Focus, 1998), 553. Cf. White, *Method and Instructions for the Art of Divine Meditation*, 14.

18. Henry Scudder, *The Christian Man's Calling* (Philadelphia: Presbyterian Board of Publication, n.d.), 103–4. Cf. William Bates, *The Whole Works of the Rev. W. Bates, D. D.*, ed. W. Farmer (repr., Harrisonburg, Va.: Sprinkle, 1990), 3:113–65.

wrote, "Study is the finding out of a truth, meditation is the spiritual improvement of a truth; the one searcheth for the vein of gold, the other digs out the gold. Study is like a winter sun that hath little warmth and influence: meditation…melts the heart when it is frozen, and makes it drop into tears of love."[19]

THE DUTY AND NECESSITY OF MEDITATION

The Puritans stressed the need for meditation. They said that, first, our God who commands us to believe commands us to meditate on His Word. That should be sufficient reason alone. They cite numerous biblical texts (Deut. 6:7; 32:46; Pss. 19:14; 49:3; 63:3; 94:19; 119:11, 15, 23, 28, 93, 99; 143:5; Isa. 1:3; Luke 2:19; 4:4; John 4:24; Eph. 1:18; 1 Tim. 4:13; Heb. 3:1) and examples (Melchizedek, Isaac, Moses, Joshua, David, Mary, Paul, Timothy). When we fail to meditate, we slight God and His Word and reveal that we are not godly (Ps. 1:2).

Second, we should meditate on the Word as a letter God has written to us. "We must not run it over in haste, but meditate upon God's wisdom in inditing, and his love in sending it to us," wrote Thomas Watson.[20] Such meditation will kindle our affections and love for God. As David said, "My hands also will I

---

19. Thomas Watson, *Gleanings from Thomas Watson* (Morgan, Pa.: Soli Deo Gloria, 1995), 106.

20. Watson, *Sermons*, 238.

lift up unto thy commandments, which I have loved; and I will meditate in thy statutes" (Ps. 119:48).

Third, one cannot be a solid Christian without meditating. As Thomas Manton said, "Faith is lean and ready to starve unless it be fed with continual meditation on the promises; as David saith, Ps. cxix. 92, 'Unless thy law had been my delight, I should then have perished in my affliction.'"[21] Watson wrote, "A Christian without meditation is like a soldier without arms, or a workman without tools. Without meditation, the truths of God will not stay with us; the heart is hard, and the memory slippery, and without meditation all is lost."[22]

Fourth, without meditation, the preached Word will fail to profit us. Reading without meditation is like swallowing "raw and undigested food," wrote Henry Scudder (c. 1585–1652).[23] Richard Baxter added, "A man may eat too much but he cannot digest too well."[24]

Watson wrote,

> There is as much difference between the knowledge of a truth, and the meditation of a truth, as there is between the light of a torch, and the light of the sun: set up a lamp or torch in the garden, and

---

21. Manton, *Works*, 17:270.

22. Watson, *Sermons*, 238.

23. Henry Scudder, *The Christian's Daily Walk, in Holy Security and Peace*, 6th ed. (1635; repr., Harrisonburg, Va.: Sprinkle, 1984), 108.

24. Baxter, *Saints' Everlasting Rest*, 549.

it hath no influence. The sun hath a sweet influence, it makes the plants to grow, and the herbs to flourish: so knowledge is but like a torch lighted in the understanding, which hath little or no influence, it makes not a man the better; but meditation is like the shining of the sun, it operates upon the affections, it warms the heart and makes it more holy. Meditation fetcheth life in a truth.[25]

Fifth, without meditation, our prayers will be less effective. As Manton wrote, "Meditation is a middle sort of duty between the word and prayer, and hath respect to both. The word feedeth meditation, and meditation feedeth prayer; we must hear that we be not erroneous, and meditate that we be not barren. These duties must always go hand in hand; meditation must follow hearing and precede prayer."[26]

Sixth, Christians who fail to meditate are unable to defend the truth. They have no backbone. And they have little self-knowledge. As Manton wrote, "A man that is a stranger to meditation is a stranger to himself."[27] "It is meditation that makes a Christian," said Watson.[28] "Thus you see the necessity of meditation," wrote Archbishop James Ussher (1581–1656).

---

25. Watson, *Sermons*, 239.

26. Manton, *Works*, 17:272.

27. Manton, *Works*, 17:271.

28. Watson, *Sermons*, 240.

"We must resolve upon the duty, if ever we mean to go to heaven."[29]

Finally, it may also be added that such meditation is an essential part of sermon preparation. Without it, sermons will lack depth of understanding, richness of feeling, and clarity of application. Johann Albrecht Bengel's (1687–1752) directive to students of the Greek New Testament captures the essence of such meditation: "Apply your whole self to the text; the whole matter of it, apply to yourself."[30]

THE MANNER OF MEDITATION

For Puritan authors, there were requisites and rules for meditation. Let us consider what they wrote about the frequency and time of meditation, preparation for meditation, and guidelines for meditation.

Frequency and Time

First, divine meditation must be frequent—ideally, twice a day, if time and obligations permit; certainly, at least once a day. If Joshua, as a busy commander, was ordered by God to meditate on His law day and night, shouldn't we also delight in meditating on God's truth every morning and evening? Generally

---

29. James Ussher, *A Method for Meditation: or, A Manuall of Divine Duties, Fit for Every Christians Practice* (London: for Joseph Nevill, 1656), 21.

30. Johann Albrecht Bengel, *New Testament Word Studies* (Grand Rapids: Kregel, 1971), 1:xxxix.

speaking, the more frequently we meditate on the triune God and His truth, the more intimately we will know Him. Meditation will also become easier.[31]

Lengthy intervals between meditations will hinder their fruit. As William Bates (1625–1699) wrote,

> If the bird leaves her nest for a long space, the eggs chill and are not fit for production; but where there is a constant incubation, then they bring forth: so when we leave religious duties for a long space, our affections chill, and grow cold; and are not fit to produce holiness, and comfort to our souls.[32]

Second, set a time for meditation and stick to that time, the Puritans advised. That will put brackets around duty and defend you "against many temptations to omission," wrote Baxter.[33] Let it be the most "seasonable time" for you, when you are most alert and not stressed by other obligations. Early morning is an excellent time because your meditations then will set the tone for the remainder of the day (Ex. 23:19; Job 1:5; Ps. 119:147; Prov. 6:22; Mark 1:35). Still, for some, evenings may be more fruitful (Gen. 24:63; Ps. 4:4). The busyness of the day is behind them, and they are ready to rest in "the bosom of God by sweet meditation"[34] (Ps. 16:7).

---

31. Calamy, *Art of Divine Meditation*, 96–101.

32. Bates, *Works*, 3:124–25.

33. Baxter, *Saints' Everlasting Rest*, 555.

34. Bates, *Works*, 3:126–27. Thomas Watson makes the strongest case for morning meditations (*Sermons of Thomas Watson*, 250–54).

Use the Lord's Day for generous doses of meditation time. In their *Directory for the Publique Worship of God*, the Westminster divines advised "that what time is vacant, between, or after the solemn meeting of the congregation in public, be spent in reading, meditation, and repetition of sermons."[35] Thomas Gouge admonished, "Had you ever tasted of the sweetness of this duty of Divine Meditation, you would find little time for vain talk, and idle discourses, especially upon the Lords day."[36] Baxter asked, "What fitter day to ascend to heaven than that on which our Lord did arise from earth, and fully triumph over death and hell, and take possession of heaven for us?"[37]

Use special times as well for meditation. Richard Baxter suggests the following: "when God doth extraordinarily revive and enable thy spirit," and "when thou art cast into perplexing troubles of mind, through sufferings, or fear, or care, or temptations." He added, third, "When the messengers of God do summon us to die; when either our grey hairs, or our languishing bodies, or some such-like forerunners of death, do tell us that our change cannot be far off."[38] William Fenner observed that a good time for

---

35. See [Westminster divines], "Of the Sanctification of the Lord's Day," in *Directory for the Publique Worship of God* (London: T. R. and E. M. for the Company of Stationers, 1651).

36. Gouge, *Christian Directions*, 66–67.

37. Baxter, *Saints' Everlasting Rest*, 560.

38. Baxter, *Saints' Everlasting Rest*, 561–63.

meditation is "when the heart is touched at a Sermon or Sacrament, or observing of any judgment or mercy, or act of Gods providence, [for then] it is best striking when the Iron is hot (Ps. 119:23)."[39] Finally, Thomas Manton suggested meditation "before some solemn duties, as before the Lord's supper, and before special times of deep humiliation, or before the Sabbath."[40]

Third, meditate "ordinarily till thou dost find some sensible benefit conveyed to thy soul." Bates said that meditating is like trying to build a fire from wet wood. Those who persevere will produce a flame. When we begin to meditate, we may first garner only a bit of smoke, then perhaps a few sparks, "but at last there is a flame of holy affections that goes up towards God." Persevere "till the flame doth so ascend," Bates said.[41]

There will be times when the flame does not ascend. You must not then carry on indefinitely. "Neither yield to laziness, nor occasion spiritual weariness: the devil hath advantage upon you both ways," Manton wrote. "When you torture your spirits after they have been spent, it makes the work of God a bondage."[42]

---

39. William Fenner, *The Use and Benefit of Divine Meditation* (London: for John Stafford, 1657), 10.

40. Manton, *Works*, 17:298.

41. Bates, *Works*, 3:125.

42. Manton, *Works*, 17:299.

Most Puritans did not advise a specific amount of time to be spent on meditation. However, James Ussher recommended at least one hour per week, and Thomas White suggested,

> considering the parts of Meditation are so many, viz. Preparation, Considerations, Affections, Resolutions, &c. and none of them are to be passed slightly over, for Affections are not so quickly raised, nor are we to cease blowing the fire as soon as ever it beginneth to flame, until it be well kindled, half an hour [each day] may be thought to be the least for beginners, and an hour for those that are versed in this duty.[43]

Preparation

Puritan writers suggested several ways to prepare for effective meditation, all of which depend "much on the frame of thy heart." First, *clear your heart from things of this world*—its business and enjoyments as well as its internal troubles and agitations. Calamy wrote, "Pray unto God not only to keep out outward company, but inward company; that is, to keep out vain, and worldly, and distracting thoughts."[44]

Second, *have your heart cleansed from the guilt and pollution of sin and stirred up with fervent love for spiritual things*. Treasure up a stock of scriptural texts and spiritual truths. Seek grace to live out David's

---

43. Ussher, *Method for Meditation*, 30–31; White, *Method and Instructions for the Art of Divine Meditation*, 29.

44. Calamy, *Art of Divine Meditation*, 173.

confession in Psalm 119:11: "Thy Word have I hid in mine heart, that I might not sin against thee."

Third, *approach the task of meditation with utmost seriousness*. Be aware of its weightiness, excellence, and potential. If you succeed, you will be admitted into the very presence of God and feel once again the beginning of eternal joy here on earth (Heidelberg Catechism 58). As Ussher wrote,

> This must be the thought of thy heart, I have to do with a God, before whom all things are naked, and bare, and therefore I must be careful to not speak foolishly before the wise God, that my thoughts be not wandering. A man may talk with the greatest Prince on earth, his mind otherwise busied; not so come to talk with God; his eye is on the heart, and therefore thy chief care must be to keep the rudder of thy heart steady. Consider the three persons in the Trinity are present.[45]

Fourth, *find a place for meditation that is quiet and free from interruption*. Aim for "secrecy, silence, rest, whereof the first excludeth company, the second noise, the third motion," wrote Joseph Hall.[46] Once a suitable place is found, stick with that place. Some Puritans recommended keeping the room dark or closing one's eyes to remove all visible distractions. Others recommended walking or sitting in the midst of nature. Here one must find his own way.

---

45. Ussher, *Method for Meditation*, 32–33.

46. Huntley, *Hall and Protestant Meditation*, 80–81.

Finally, *maintain a body posture that is reverent, whether it be sitting, standing, walking, or lying prostrate before the Almighty.* While meditating, the body should be the servant of the soul, following its affections. The goal is to center the soul, the mind, and the body on "the glory of God in the face of Jesus Christ" (2 Cor. 4:6).[47]

Guidelines

The Puritans also offered guidelines for the process of meditation. They said to begin by asking the Holy Spirit for assistance. Pray for the power to harness your mind and to focus the eyes of faith on this task. As Calamy wrote,

> I would have you pray unto God to enlighten your understandings, to quicken your devotion, to warm your affections, and so to bless that hour unto you, that by the meditation of holy things you may be made more holy, you may have your lusts more mortified, and your graces more increased, you may be the more mortified to the world, and the vanity of it, and lifted up to Heaven, and the things of Heaven.[48]

Next, the Puritans said to read the Scriptures, then select a verse or doctrine on which to meditate. Be sure to pick out relatively easy subjects to meditate on at the beginning. For example, begin with the

---

47. Bates, *Works*, 136–39; Baxter, *Saints' Everlasting Rest*, 567–70.

48. Calamy, *Art of Divine Meditation*, 172.

attributes of God rather than the doctrine of the Trinity, and consider subjects one at a time.

In addition, select subjects that are most applicable to your present circumstances and that will be most beneficial for your soul. For example, if you're spiritually dejected, meditate on Christ's willingness to receive poor sinners and pardon all who come to Him. If your conscience troubles you, meditate on God's promises to give grace to the penitent. If you're financially afflicted, meditate on God's wonderful providences to those in need.[49] Now, memorize the selected verse(s) or some aspect of the subject to stimulate meditation, strengthen faith, and serve as a means of divine guidance.

Next, fix your thoughts on the Scripture or a scriptural subject without prying further than what God has revealed. Use your memory to focus on all that Scripture has to say about your subject. Consider past sermons and other edifying books. Use "the book of conscience, the book of Scripture, and the book of the creature"[50] as you consider various aspects of your subject: its names, causes, qualities, fruits, and effects. Like Mary, ponder these things in your heart. Think of illustrations, similitudes, and opposites in your mind to enlighten your understanding and enflame

---

49. Calamy, *Art of Divine Meditation*, 164–68.

50. George Swinnock, *The Works of George Swinnock* (Edinburgh: Banner of Truth Trust, 1998), 2:417.

your affections. Then let judgment assess the value of what you are meditating on.

Here's an example from Calamy. If you would meditate on the subject of sin, "begin with the description of sin; proceed to the distribution of sin; consider the original and cause of sin, the cursed fruits and effects of sin, the adjuncts and properties of sin in general and of personal sin in particular, the opposite of sin—grace, the metaphors of sin, the titles given to sin, [and] all that the Scripture saith concerning sin."[51]

Two warnings are in order. First, as Manton wrote, "do not bridle up the free spirit by the rules of method. That which God calleth for is religion, not logic. When Christians confine themselves to such rules and prescriptions, they straiten themselves, and thoughts come from them like water out of a still, not like water out of a fountain."[52] Second, if your mind wanders, rein it in, offer a short prayer for forgiveness, ask for strength to stay focused, read a few appropriate Scriptures again, and press on. Remember, reading Scripture, meditation, and prayer belong together. As one discipline wanes, turn to another. Persevere; don't surrender to Satan by abandoning your task.

---

51. Calamy, *Art of Divine Meditation*, 178–84. Cf. Gouge, *Christian Directions*, 70–73.

52. Manton, *Works*, 17:281.

Next, stir up affections, such as love, desire, hope, courage, gratitude, zeal, and joy,[53] to glorify God.[54] Hold soliloquies with your own soul. Include complaints against yourself because of your inabilities and shortcomings, and spread before God your spiritual longings. Believe that He will help you.

In discussing meditations as a "private means" of grace, Paul Baynes (1573–1617) compared it first with the power of sight to affect the heart, then with the process of conception and birth: "Now look as after conception, there is a travail to bring forth & a birth in due season: so when the soul by thought hath conceived, presently the affections are tickled and excited, for the affections kindle on a thought, as tinder doth, when a spark lighteth on it. The affections moved, the will is stirred and inclined."[55]

Now, following the arousal of your memory, judgment, and affections, apply your meditations to yourself to arouse your soul to duty and comfort and to restrain your soul from sin.[56] As William Fenner (1600–1640) wrote, "Dive into thy own soul; anticipate and prevent thy own heart. Haunt thy heart with promises, threatenings, mercies, judgments,

---

53. Baxter, *Saints' Everlasting Rest*, 579–90.

54. Jonathan Edwards, *Religious Affections* (London: Banner of Truth Trust, 1959), 24.

55. Paul Baynes, *A Help to True Happinesse* (London: R. Y[oung] for Edward Brewster, 1635).

56. Bates, *Works*, 3:145.

and commandments. Let meditation trace [out] thy heart."[57]

Examine yourself for your own growth in grace. Reflect on the past and ask, "What have I done?" Look to the future, asking, "What am I resolved to do, by God's grace?"[58] Do not ask such questions legalistically but out of holy excitement and opportunity to grow in Spirit-worked grace. Remember, "Legal work is our work; meditation work is sweet work."[59]

Follow Calamy's advice: "If ever you would get good by the practice of meditation, you must come down to *particulars*; and you must so meditate of Christ, as to apply Christ to thy soul; and so meditate of Heaven, as to apply Heaven to thy soul."[60] Live out your meditation (Josh. 1:8). Let meditation and practice, like two sisters, walk hand in hand. Meditation without practice will only increase your condemnation.[61]

Next, turn your applications into resolutions. "Let your resolutions be firm and strong, not [mere] wishes, but resolved purposes or Determinations," wrote White. Make your resolutions commitments to fight against your temptations to sin. Write down

---

57. Fenner, *Use and Benefit of Divine Meditation*, 16–23.

58. Ussher, *Method for Meditation*, 39.

59. William Bridge, *The Works of the Rev. William Bridge* (1845; repr., Beaver Falls, Pa.: Soli Deo Gloria, 1989), 3:153.

60. Calamy, *Art of Divine Meditation*, 108.

61. Watson, *Sermons*, 269, 271.

your resolutions. Above all, resolve that you will spend your life "as becomes one that hath been meditating of holy and heavenly things." Commend yourself, your family, and everything you own to the hands of God with "sweet resignation."[62]

Conclude with prayer, thanksgiving, and psalm singing. "Meditation is the best beginning of prayer, and prayer is the best conclusion of meditation," wrote George Swinnock (c. 1627–1673). Watson said,

> Pray over your meditations. Prayer sanctifies every thing; without prayer they are but unhallowed meditations; prayer fastens meditation upon the soul; prayer is a tying a knot at the end of meditation that it doth not slip; pray that God will keep those holy meditations in your mind for ever, that the savour of them may abide upon your hearts.[63]

Thank the Lord for assistance in meditation, or else, Richard Greenham (c. 1542–1594) warned, "we shall be buffeted in our next meditation."[64]

The metrical versions of the Psalms are a great help in meditation. Their metrical form facilitates memorization. As God's Word, they are a proper subject for meditation. Calvin referred to them as a "complete anatomy of the soul," affording abundant material and guidance for meditation. As prayers (Ps. 72:20) and as thanksgiving (Ps. 118:1), they are

---

62. White, *Method and Instructions for the Art of Divine Meditation*, 53.

63. Watson, *Sermons*, 269.

64. Greenham, *Works*, 41.

both a proper vehicle for meditation and a fitting way to conclude it. Joseph Hall wrote that he found much comfort in closing his meditations by lifting up his "heart and voice to God in singing some verse or two of David's Psalms—one that answers to our disposition and the matter of our meditation. In this way, the heart closes up with much sweetness and contentment."[65] John Lightfoot (1602–1675) added, "Singing God's praise is a work of the most meditation of any we perform in public. It keeps the heart longest upon the thing spoken. Prayer and hearing pass quick from one sentence to another; this sticks long upon it."

Finally, don't shift too quickly from meditation to engagement with things of this world, lest, as Thomas Gouge advised, "thereby thou suddenly quench that spiritual heat which hath in that exercise been kindled in thine heart."[66] Remember that one hour spent in such meditation is "worth more than a thousand sermons," Ussher said, "and this is no debasing of the Word, but an honour to it."[67]

THE SUBJECTS OF MEDITATION

The Puritans suggested various subjects, objects, and materials for meditation. Some of the most

---

65. Joseph Hall, *The Art of Meditation* (Jenkintown, Pa.: Sovereign Grace Publishers, 1972), 26–27.

66. Gouge, *Christian Directions*, 70.

67. Ussher, *Method for Meditation*, 43.

common were the divine qualities of the Word of God, the attributes and works of God, the sinfulness of sin and corruption of our hearts, the mortality and vanity of man, the person and work of Christ, the promises of God, the person and work of the Holy Spirit, the experiential marks of grace in our lives, death, judgment, hell, and—most of all—heaven and eternal glory.

Clearly for the Puritans, some topics ought to be more focused on than others. That led John Owen to say, "If I have observed anything by experience, it is this: a man may take the measure of his growth and decay in grace according to his thoughts and meditations upon the person of Christ, and the glory of Christ's kingdom, and of His love."[68]

For the Puritans, probably the most important theme for meditation was heaven—the place where God is supremely known and worshiped and enjoyed, where Christ is seated at the right hand of the Father, and where the saints rejoice as they are transcribed from glory to glory. "Meditation is the life of most other duties: and the views of heaven is the life of Meditation," wrote Baxter.[69] Heaven was the supreme subject for meditation for these reasons:

---

68. Quoted in John Blanchard, *The Complete Gathered Gold* (Darlington, U.K.: Evangelical Press, 2006), 409.

69. Baxter, *Saints' Everlasting Rest*, 702.

- Christ is in heaven now, and our salvation consists of union through the Holy Spirit with Christ. He is our wisdom, righteousness, sanctification, and redemption. Christ, the center of heaven, ought to be the center of all our faith, hope, and love.

- We can live as Christians in the present evil age only if we have the mind of Christ—that is, if we are genuinely heavenly-minded, seeing our earth and this age from the perspective of heaven.

- Heaven is the goal of our pilgrimage. We are pilgrims on the earth, journeying in faith, hope, and love toward heaven to be with Christ.[70]

The Puritans taught that meditations on heaven and other subjects take priority on three occasions. First, special meditation is necessary in conjunction with worship, particularly with regard to the sermon. "God requires you to hear Sermons, requires you to meditate on the Sermons you hear," wrote

---

70. Peter Toon, *From Mind to Heart: Christian Meditation Today* (Grand Rapids: Baker, 1987), 95–96. For how to meditate on heaven, see White, *Method and Instructions for the Art of Divine Meditation*, 281–94; Baxter, *Saints' Everlasting Rest*, 620–52; and Thomas Case, *The Select Works of Thomas Case* (Ligonier, Pa.: Soli Deo Gloria, 1993), 1–232 (second book).

Calamy.[71] As James Ussher wrote, "Every sermon is but a preparation for meditation."[72]

Good sermons not only inform the mind with sound doctrine but also stir up the affections. They turn the will away from sin and toward loving God and one's neighbor. Meditation enlarges and directs the affections through the reception of the Word of God in the heart from the mind. When people stop meditating on sermons, they stop benefiting from them.

Baxter wrote, "Why so much preaching is lost among us, and professors can run from sermon to sermon, and are never weary of hearing or reading, and yet have such languishing, starved souls, I know no truer or greater cause than their ignorance and unconscionable neglect of meditation." Some hearers have anorexia, Baxter said, for "they have neither appetite nor digestion," but others have bulimia— "they have appetite, but no digestion."[73]

Conscientious Puritans often took sermon notes to help facilitate meditation. In my own congregation, an elderly Christian woman decided to emulate that practice. Every Sabbath evening she spent an hour on her knees with notes from the sermons of the day, praying and meditating her way through them. She often said that was the best part of her Sabbath.

---

71. Calamy, *Art of Divine Meditation*, 4.

72. Ussher, *Method for Meditation*, 49.

73. Baxter, *Saints' Everlasting Rest*, 549–50.

Second, to rightly receive the sacrament of the Lord's Supper, a believer is expected to meditate on the Lord Jesus as sacrifice for his sin. As Thomas White wrote,

Meditate upon your preparatory, concomitant and subsequent duties: Meditate upon the love of God the Father, upon the love of God the Son, Jesus Christ, consider the excellency of his person, the greatness of his sufferings, and how valid they be to the satisfaction of Gods Justice, and so likewise to consider of the excellency, nature, and use of the Sacrament.[74]

Calamy listed twelve subjects for meditations during the sacrament:

The great and wonderful love of God the Father in giving Christ; the love of Christ in giving himself; the heinousness of sin; the excellency of this Sacramental feast; your own unworthiness; your spiritual wants and necessities; the cursed condition of an unworthy receiver; the happy condition of those that come worthily; the Sacramental Elements [bread and wine]; the Sacramental actions [how the minister's actions represent Christ]; the Sacramental Promises; what retribution to make unto Christ for [the gift of His Supper].[75]

Some Puritan divines, such as Edward Reynolds (1599–1676), wrote entire treatises to help believers

---

74. White, *Method and Instructions for the Art of Divine Meditation*, 88.

75. Calamy, *Art of Divine Meditation*, 88–96. Cf. Manton, *Works*, 17:288–97.

during the Lord's Supper.[76] John Owen showed how preparation for the Lord's Supper involved meditation, examination, supplication, and expectation.[77] Every believer was expected to share in that preparation (cf. Westminster Larger Catechism, Q. 171, 174, 175).

Third, every Sabbath was a special season for meditation. It was a time of spiritual nourishment for the God-fearing who stocked up on spiritual goods for the week to come. Hence the Sabbath was fondly called "the market day of the soul."

Finally, Puritans such as Nathanael Ranew (c. 1602–1677), who wrote extensively on meditation, gave various directions to believers, depending on their spiritual maturity. Ranew wrote chapters for "young Christians newly converted," "more grown and elder Christians," and for "old Christians." The older the Christian, the greater the expectation for more profound meditations.[78]

76. Edward Reynolds, "Meditation on the Holy Sacrament of the Lord's Last Supper," in *The Whole Works of the Right Rev. Edward Reynolds* (Morgan, Pa.: Soli Deo Gloria, 1999), 3:1–172.

77. John Owen, *The Works of John Owen*, ed. William H. Goold (repr., Edinburgh: Banner of Truth Trust, 1999), 9:558–63.

78. Nathanael Ranew, *Solitude Improved by Divine Meditation* (Morgan, Pa.: Soli Deo Gloria, 1995), 280–321.

THE BENEFITS OF MEDITATION

The Puritans devoted scores of pages to the benefits, excellence, usefulness, advantages, or improvements of meditation. Here are some of those benefits:

- Meditation helps us focus on the triune God, to love and to enjoy Him in all His persons (1 John 4:8)—intellectually, spiritually, aesthetically.

- Meditation helps increase knowledge of sacred truth. It "takes the veil from the face of truth" (cf. Prov. 4:2).

- Meditation is the "nurse of wisdom," for it promotes the fear of God, which is the beginning of wisdom (cf. Prov. 1:7).

- Meditation enlarges our faith by helping us to trust the God of promises in all our spiritual troubles and the God of providence in all our outward troubles.[79]

- Meditation augments one's affections. Watson called meditation "the bellows of the affections." He said, "Meditation hatcheth good affections, as the hen her young ones by sitting on them; we light affection at this fire of meditation"[80] (Ps. 39:3).

---

79. Calamy, *Art of Divine Meditation*, 40–42.
80. Watson, *Sermons*, 256.

- Meditation fosters repentance and reformation of life (Ps. 119:59; Ezek. 36:31).

- Meditation is a great friend to memory.

- Meditation helps us view worship as a discipline to be cultivated. It makes us prefer God's house to our own.

- Meditation transfuses Scripture through the texture of the soul.

- Meditation is a great aid to prayer (Ps. 5:1). It tunes the instrument of prayer before prayer.

- Meditation helps us to hear and read the Word with real benefit. It makes the Word "full of life and energy to our souls." William Bates wrote, "Hearing the word is like ingestion, and when we meditate upon the word that is digestion; and this digestion of the word by meditation produceth warm affections, zealous resolutions, and holy actions."[81]

- Meditation on the sacraments helps our graces to be better and stronger. It helps faith, hope, love, humility, and numerous spiritual comforts thrive in the soul.

- Meditation stresses the heinousness of sin. It "musters up all weapons, and gathers all

---

81. Bates, *Works*, 3:131.

forces of arguments for to press our sins, and lay them heavy upon the heart," wrote Fenner.[82] Thomas Hooker said, "Meditation sharpens the sting and strength of corruption, that it pierceth more prevailingly."[83] It is a "strong antidote against sin" and "a cure of covetousness."

- Meditation enables us to "discharge religious duties, because it conveys to the soul the lively sense and feeling of God's goodness; so the soul is encouraged to duty."[84]

- Meditation helps prevent vain and sinful thoughts (Jer. 4:14; Matt. 12:35). It helps wean us from this present evil age.

- Meditation provides inner resources on which to draw (Ps. 77:10–12), including direction for daily life (Prov. 6:21–22).

- Meditation helps us persevere in faith; it keeps our hearts "savoury and spiritual in the midst of all our outward and worldly employments," wrote William Bridge.[85]

- Meditation is a mighty weapon to ward off Satan and temptation (Ps. 119:11, 15; 1 John 2:14).

---

82. Fenner, *Use and Benefit of Divine Meditation*, 3.

83. Hooker, *Application of Redemption*, 217.

84. Bates, *Works*, 3:135.

85. Bridge, *Works*, 3:133.

- Meditation provides relief in afflictions (Isa. 49:15–17; Heb. 12:5).

- Meditation helps us benefit others with our spiritual fellowship and counsel (Ps. 66:16; 77:12; 145:7).

- Meditation promotes gratitude for all the blessings showered on us by God through His Son.

- Meditation glorifies God (Ps. 49:3).[86]

In short, as Thomas Brooks (1608–1680) wrote, "meditation is the food of your souls, it is the very stomach and natural heat whereby spiritual truths are digested. A man shall as soon live without his heart, as he shall be able to get good by what he reads, without meditation…. It is not he that reads most; but he that meditates most, that will prove the choicest, sweetest, wisest, and strongest Christian."[87]

THE OBSTACLES TO MEDITATION

Puritan leaders frequently warned people about hindrances or obstacles to meditation. Here is a summary of their responses to such obstacles:

---

86. Cf. Oliver Heywood, *The Whole Works of the Rev. Oliver Heywood* (Idle, U.K.: by John Vint for F. Westley et al., 1825), 2:276–81.

87. Brooks, *Works*, 1:8, 291.

Obstacle 1: Unfitness or ignorance. Such say they cannot confine their thoughts to a particular subject. Their "thoughts are light and feathery, tossed to and fro."

Answer: Disability, ignorance, and wandering thoughts offer no exemption from duty. Your "loss of ability" does not imply God's "loss of right." Truth be told, you are probably unfit because you have neglected meditation and have not loved the truth. "Sinful indispositions do not disannul our engagements to God, as a servant's drunkenness doth not excuse him from work," Manton wrote. Remedy your problem by getting "a good stock of sanctified knowledge" and by "constant exercise" of that knowledge, all the while leaning on the Holy Spirit for assistance. You will find meditation becoming easier and sweeter in due course.[88]

Obstacle 2: Busyness. Such say they are so harassed by this world's responsibilities that they cannot find time to engage seriously in meditation.

Answer: True religion is not performed merely in leisure time. Great busyness should move us to more meditation, as we then have more needs to bring before God and to meditate on.

---

88. Manton, *Works*, 6:145.

Obstacle 3: Spiritual lethargy. Such admit that though they may have good intentions, their soul is prone to divert itself from meditation.

Answer: Matthew 11:12 says heaven is the reward of "the violent [who] take it by force." Why are you lazy in spiritual pursuits that can reap eternal rewards when you are not lazy in pursuing secular work in this world, which produces only temporary rewards? Spiritual "drowsiness shall clothe a man with rags" (Prov. 23:21). As Manton said, "It is better to take pains than to suffer pains, and to be bound with the cords of duty than with the chains of darkness."[89]

Obstacle 4: Worldly pleasures and friendships. Such say they don't want to be righteous overmuch and hence do not wish to abandon vain entertainment and friends.

Answer: "The pleasures of the world discompose our souls, and unfit our bodies for the duties of meditation…. Remember this, the sweetness of religion is incomparably more than all the pleasures of sense," wrote Bates.[90]

Obstacle 5: Adverseness of heart. Such say they don't like to be yoked to such a difficult task. Burdened with guilt, they fear being alone with God.

---

89. Manton, *Works*, 17:283.

90. Bates, *Works*, 3:122–23.

Answer: "Get your conscience cleansed by the hearty application of the blood of Christ," Manton advised, then yoke yourself to the means of grace, including meditation (Ps. 19:14).[91]

The consequences of omitting meditation are serious, Calamy warned. It leads to hardness of heart. Why do the promises and threatenings of God make so little impression on us? It's because we fail to meditate on them. Why are we so ungrateful to God for His blessings? Why do His providences and afflictions fail to produce godly fruit in our lives? Why do we fail to benefit from the Word and sacraments, why are we so judgmental of others, why do we so feebly prepare for eternity? Isn't it largely due to our lack of meditation?[92]

Most Puritan pastors said that we must discipline ourselves to meditate. Yet comparatively few people, even in Puritan times, saw this as their duty. "Many are troubled," wrote Baxter, "if they omit a sermon, a fast, a prayer in public or private, yet were never troubled that they have omitted meditation, perhaps all their life-time to this very day."[93]

---

91. Manton, *Works*, 17:285. Cf. Hooker, *Application of Redemption*, 230–40.

92. Calamy, *Art of Divine Meditation*, 28–40.

93. Baxter, *Saints' Everlasting Rest*, 549.

CONCLUSION: SELF-EXAMINATION

Puritan meditation was more than a particular means of grace; it was a comprehensive method for Puritan devotion—a biblical, doctrinal, experiential, and practical art. Its theology was Pauline, Augustinian, and Calvinistic. Its subject matter was drawn from the book of Scripture, the book of creation, and the book of conscience. As Bridge said, "Meditation is the vehement or intense application of the soul unto some thing, whereby a man's mind doth ponder, dwell and fix upon it, for his own profit and benefit," which, in turn, leads to God's glory.[94]

Typically, Puritans concluded their treatises on meditation by calling readers to self-examination, which consists of trial and reproof, or exhortation. Trial involves the following considerations:

- Are your meditations motivated by the exercise of a "lively faith"? Real meditation is inseparable from the exercise of faith. Do you ever meditate as Samuel Ward (1577–1640) describes: "Stir up thy soul in [meditation] to converse with Christ. Look what promises and privileges thou dost habitually believe, now actually think of them, roll them under thy tongue, chew on them till thou feel some sweetness in the palate of thy soul. View them jointly, severally: sometimes muse on one, sometimes of

---

94. Bridge, *Works*, 3:125.

another more deeply. This is that which the Spouse calls walking into the Gardens and eating of the Fruits, which in plain terms, I call using of Faith, and living by Faith."[95]

- "Are these spiritual thoughts in thy heart, productive of holiness in thy life?" Remember, "to be weary of the thoughts of God is to degenerate into devils"[96] (cf. James 2:19).

Reproof, or exhortation, reflects on the following factors:

- For the unbeliever: When God made you a rational creature, did He intend that you should use your thoughts for selfish and sinful purposes? Why isn't God in all your thoughts? "Hast thou not a God and a Christ to think of? And is not salvation by him, and everlasting glory, worthy of your choicest thoughts? You have thoughts enough and to spare for other things—for base things, for very toys—and why not for God and the word of God?" Manton asked.[97]

- For the believer: Neglecting meditation should "strike us with fear and sorrow." How degrading it is to God when we turn

95. Samuel Ward, *Collection of Sermons and Treatises* (London, 1636), 69–70.

96. Manton, *Works*, 7:480.

97. Manton, *Works*, 6:145.

our meditation from Him to sinful objects! If the farmer meditates on his land, the physician on his patients, the lawyer on his cases, the storeowner on his wares, shouldn't Christians meditate on their God and Savior?[98]

The Puritans would say to us,

If you continue to neglect meditation, it will dampen or destroy your love for God. It will make it unpleasant to think about God. It will leave you open to sin so that you view sin as a pleasure. It will leave you vulnerable and fragile before trials and temptations of every kind. In short, it will lead to a falling away from God.[99]

"No holy duties will come to us," Ranew wrote, "we must come to them."[100] Let us heed Watson's exhortation:

If you have formerly neglected it, bewail your neglect, and now begin to make conscience of it: lock up yourselves with God (at least once a day) by holy meditation. Ascend this hill, and when you are gotten to the top of it, you shall see a fair prospect, Christ and heaven before you. Let me put you in mind of that saying of Bernard, "O saint, knowest thou not that thy husband Christ is bashful, and will not be familiar in company, retire

---

98. Calamy, *Art of Divine Meditation*, 58–75.

99. Edmond Smith, *A Tree by a Stream: Unlock the Secrets of Active Meditation* (Fearn, Scotland: Christian Focus, 1995), 36.

100. Ranew, *Solitude Improved by Divine Meditation*, 33.

thyself by meditation into the closet, or the field, and there thou shalt have Christ's embraces."[101]

How can you begin practicing Christian meditation? Ask God to help you take this teaching of the Puritans on spiritual meditation and put it into practice. Begin today. Begin with just nine minutes a day. Read the Scriptures slowly and thoughtfully for three minutes, meditate on what you've read for three minutes, and then pray for three minutes. You will discover almost immediately that your meditation will supply you with content for your prayers. Once you learn, with the Puritans, that meditation is "the half-way house" between Scripture reading and prayer, you will not be able to stop meditating on a regular basis, and you will find your meditation time will naturally augment itself both in time and in quality. You will then not be able to restrain yourself from telling your Christian friends that spiritual meditation is one of the most important spiritual disciplines a Christian is called to engage in.

---

101. Watson, *Sermons*, 241–43.